10 STUDY GOALS

LAURA BAKER • FATTI BURKE

PowerKiDS press

Published in 2027
by The Rosen Publishing Group, Inc.
2544 Clinton Street, Buffalo, NY 14224

First published in Great Britain in 2022 by Wayland

Credits

Editor: Julia Bird

Editorial, design and project management: Raspberry Books

Design: Intrepid Books LTD

Illustrations: Fatti Burke

Cataloging-in-Publication Data

Names: Baker, Laura, 1983-, author. | Burke, Fatti, illustrator.
Title: 10 study goals / written by Laura Baker, illustrated by Fatti Burke.
Description: Buffalo, New York : PowerKids Press, 2027. | Series: 10 goals | Includes glossary and index.
Identifiers: ISBN 9781499459159 (pbk.) | ISBN 9781499459166 (library bound) | ISBN 9781499459173 (ebook)
Subjects: LCSH: Study skills--Juvenile literature. | Time management--Juvenile literature. | Academic achievement--Juvenile literature.
Classification: LCC LB1049.B35 2027 | DDC 371.30281--dc23

Printed in China

CPSIA Compliance Information: Batch #QS27PK. For further information contact Rosen Publishing at 1-800-237-9932.

CONTENTS

Learn top studyingskills - and set yourself up for life.

WHY STUDY GOALS ARE GOOD

There is so much more to studying than simply sitting down at a desk to work.

To get the most out of your study time, you need to be in the right frame of mind, in a good spot to focus and with the perfect plan to make it a properly useful session.

When studying begins to feel like a chore, or you're too tired or distracted to work, you can end up working for an hour without getting very far at all. But when studying is a habit, and your mind is clear, that same hour can get you so much further.

So, do you want to know the secret? It's not always about studying hard or studying lots. It's about studying SMART.

Set yourself these 10 study goals to learn how to study smart at home, and in school too.

GOAL 1

DITCH DISTRACTIONS

For example:
When you're feeling upset or anxious, your mind can't focus as well as it should.

WHEN YOUR FAMILY IS HAVING A CONVERSATION AROUND YOU, YOU MIGHT BE TEMPTED TO JOIN IN.

When a phone lights up, it steals your attention from what you're doing. Even when the phone isn't distracting you, the fact that it's sitting next to you means that it could — and your mind is aware of this.

You can hear the TV.

THE MORE INTERRUPTIONS THERE ARE, THE LONGER IT WILL TAKE TO STUDY AND THE LESS INFORMATION YOU'LL TAKE IN.

All these things can make your mind wander.

Remember:
Bring distractions down, and your studying will go up!

TOP TIPS TO DITCH YOUR DISTRACTIONS

Distractions will never go away completely. Your mind might wander by itself, without anything to prompt it! But if you can keep disruptions to a minimum, you can get your thoughts on track.

1 PUT THEM OUT OF REACH!

TURN OFF ALL YOUR DEVICES (PHONE, TABLET, TV, ETC.), OR LEAVE THEM IN A SEPARATE ROOM IF YOU CAN. IF YOU'RE WORKING ON A COMPUTER OR TABLET, CLOSE ANY SOCIAL MEDIA APPS OR WINDOWS THAT AREN'T RELATED TO YOUR WORK. GIVE YOURSELF A SMALL, SOLID CHUNK OF TIME TO STUDY DEVICE-FREE.

2 GET IN THE ZONE

Find a peaceful area in your home where you can concentrate and avoid becoming distracted. If you use music to help you focus, consider putting on headphones. This keeps the music in your ears and drowns out any other sounds.

3 CLEAR YOUR MIND

DO YOUR BEST TO GET ENOUGH SLEEP – AIM FOR 10 TO 11 HOURS A NIGHT. EAT HEALTHY BRAIN FOOD, SUCH AS FRUITS AND VEGETABLES, FISH, NUTS AND SEEDS. THIS WILL KEEP YOUR BRAIN ALERT AND YOUR BODY ENERGIZED. TAKE DEEP BREATHS TO CLEAR YOUR MIND IF YOU FIND OTHER THOUGHTS TAKING OVER.

Three ... two ... one ... Focus.

DO YOU LIKE TO WORK IN...

a) controlled chaos?
b) super silence?
c) somewhere in the middle?

Everyone is different. Create a space that works for YOU.

GOAL 2

SET UP YOUR SPACE

Think about where you study best. Do you need the buzz and support of people around you? Or do you prefer to concentrate in your own zone? Whatever your style, have that space ready to go. This way you can get straight to studying when you're ready, rather than losing time and energy setting up for each session.

THE KITCHEN-TABLE WORKER

If you answered a) above, find your own place in the chaos. Spread out at the kitchen table, but make sure you have somewhere to keep your supplies handy.

THE DESK FAN

IF YOU ANSWERED B), YOU MIGHT LIKE TO MAKE A SNUG SPACE OF YOUR OWN IN YOUR BEDROOM. FIND A CORNER OR DESK WHERE YOU CAN KEEP TO YOURSELF AND FOCUS.

THE FLOOR SPREADER-OUTER

If you answered c), you might like a more portable option. Create a carry-along caddy (see page 13) so that you can study anywhere.

TOP TIPS TO SET

Wherever you make your desk, these are some things you can do to create a helpful, practical, and inspiring study space.

1 PUT UP A NOTICE BOARD

THIS COULD BE A CORKBOARD OR A MAGNETIC WHITEBOARD – JUST SOMEWHERE TO KEEP NOTES, REMINDERS, AND SCHEDULES HANDY.

2 PLACE A CLOCK AND CALENDAR IN VIEW

Keep track of study times and stick to your studying schedule.

3 SET UP THE LIGHTING

FIND A DESK LAMP TO LIGHT YOUR WORK IF YOU NEED TO – MAKE SURE YOU'RE NOT STRUGGLING TO READ IN DIM LIGHT.

UP YOUR SPACE

4 HAVE YOUR PENS, PENCILS, AND NOTEBOOK NEARBY

If you don't have space to keep these on the table at all times, think about making a portable supply caddy (see below).

5 GET COMFY (BUT NOT TOO COMFY!)

MAKE SURE YOU HAVE A COMFORTABLE CHAIR OR CUSHION TO SIT ON, BUT DON'T SINK INTO IT SO MUCH THAT YOU'RE FALLING ASLEEP.

6 PERSONALISE

You'll have more fun studying if you're in a happy place. Decorate your space to suit you.

MAKE A CARRY-ALONG CADDY

1. Find a basket, plastic crate, or shoebox. Decorate it to make it your own!
2. Place paper cups inside.
3. Fill the cups with pencils, pens, an eraser, a pencil sharpener, and other items you're always reaching for.
4. Store it away when you're not using it. Then grab it whenever you're ready to study!

GOAL 3

MAKE IT A HABIT

Biting fingernails = bad habit.
Saying thank you when someone holds open a door for you = good habit.

Making studying a regular part of your day = very good habit!

A habit is something that you do regularly, often without even thinking about it, such as putting on a seatbelt when you get in the car or brushing your teeth before bed. Some habits are good and some are not-so-good. Once a habit is formed, it's ingrained in your brain and is very hard to break.

FORMING NEW HABITS CAN BE TRICKY, TOO. IT CAN TAKE DAYS OR EVEN MONTHS OF REPEATING AN ACTION TO TURN IT INTO SOMETHING THAT FEELS AUTOMATIC.

When you learn a new skill, you use a different part of your brain from the part you use when you do something that's automatic. When actions become habits they free up brainpower! This is good news for studying – if you turn your studying time into a habit, then you have more brain space to take in what you're actually learning.

Remember:
Regular study habit =
better studying power!

TOP TIPS TO MAKE IT A HABIT

There are a few key ingredients to turn studying into a habit that becomes just another part of your life.

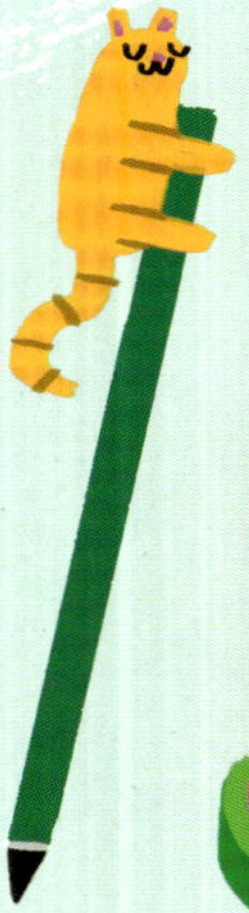

1 CHOOSE THE SAME TIME OF DAY TO STUDY

This might be straight after school, or after dinner if you need to fill your tummy first.

2 CHOOSE THE SAME TIME OF THE WEEK TO STUDY

YOU MIGHT CHOOSE TO GIVE YOURSELF THE WEEKEND OFF, BUT MAKE SURE STUDYING BECOMES A PART OF THE SAME DAYS EVERY WEEK.

3 IT'S ALL ABOUT THE ROUTINE

Fit studying into your daily routine. This makes it something that your brain expects to do, so it's no big deal to get straight into it. It also means that you know what comes next when you're done! Maybe after studying you could have a snack or watch your favorite TV show.

4 DON'T FIGHT IT!

PROCRASTINATION MEANS PUTTING SOMETHING OFF. IF YOU PROCRASTINATE WHEN YOU'RE MEANT TO BE STUDYING, IT WILL BECOME HARDER TO DO. STICK TO YOUR ROUTINE AND IT WILL BECOME A HABIT INSTEAD.

- Wake up
- Eat breakfast
- Brush teeth
- Get dressed
- Go to school
- Eat an after-school snack
- Study
- Play outside
- Eat dinner
- Quiet time
- Brush teeth
- Bath and PJs
- Go to bed

5 DON'T PANIC

If your routine changes one day because something comes up, that's OK! Don't panic. Just try to get back on schedule the next time.

GOAL 4

PLAN, DON'T CRAM

HOW DO YOU PREPARE FOR A TEST OR PROJECT? DO YOU ...

a) do small bits every day?
b) do everything all at once the night before?

If you answered a), you're well on your way to becoming a top planner. But if you answered b), you might be a last-minute crammer.

Just as you can cram all your clothes into a tiny suitcase, you can cram work into a small amount of time. But like that suitcase, which will be bursting at the seams, cramming your studying has its own problems.

STUDYING VERY QUICKLY MEANS YOU'RE MORE FOCUSED ON GETTING THE INFO INTO YOUR BRAIN THAN TAKING IT IN PROPERLY.

So while you might do well on a test the next day, you might not remember the information in the long run!

YOU USE ENERGY JUST KEEPING YOUR EYES OPEN AND YOUR BRAIN IN GEAR WHEN YOU STUDY QUICKLY. THIS IS USING UP ESSENTIAL BRAINPOWER!

Try to make it a habit to revise in small amounts over longer periods of time to get the best out of your studying.

TOP TIPS TO PLAN FOR SUCCESS

You need to own your studying. Don't let test days creep up on you! The best way to avoid cramming is to PLAN. Plan your week, plan your month, plan your success. There are several simple tools that can help:

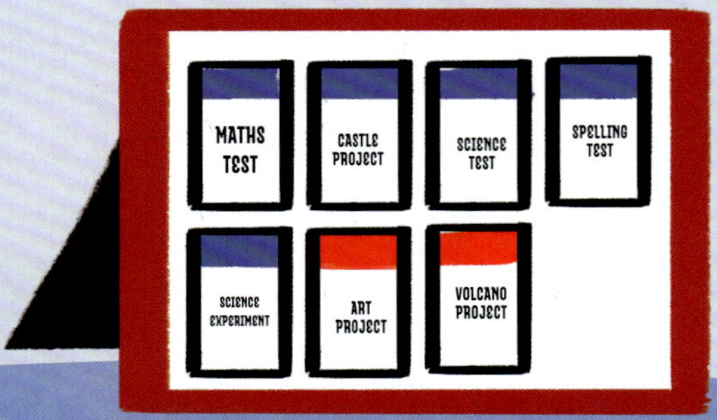

1 USE A CALENDAR

Write down important dates so you can see them. This can include tests, project due dates, or any other events you might need to prepare for. This helps you see what you have coming up, how much time you've got and how things might overlap.

2 PRIORITIZE

IF YOU HAVE LOTS OF WORK GOING ON, THINK ABOUT WHAT IS MOST URGENT OR MOST CHALLENGING. MAKE A LIST FROM MOST IMPORTANT TO LEAST IMPORTANT. KEEP UPDATING THIS LIST AS THE DAYS GO BY.

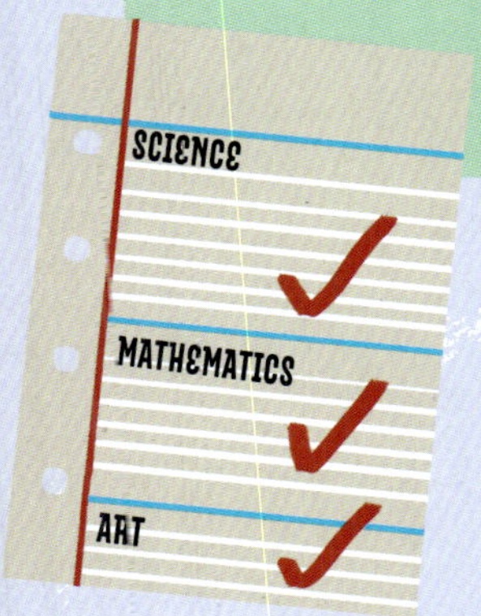

3 PLAN YOUR WEEK

Break down the work that you need to do for a test or project over the time that you have to do it in. Do small amounts in each study session so that by the end you only need to review everything rather than try to do it all.

4 USE A DAY PLANNER

THE CLUE IS IN THE NAME! A DAILY PLANNER HELPS YOU KEEP TRACK OF YOUR TIME. WRITE DOWN WHAT YOU'LL DO EACH DAY... AND THEN ENJOY CROSSING EACH ITEM OFF THE LIST WHEN YOU'VE FINISHED!

GOAL 5

REVIEW BEFORE LEARNING NEW

Have you ever learned a cool new fact, and then forgotten it completely when you went to share it with someone days later? Information can stick if you really take it in, but it can also just disappear from your mind if you don't.

Just like cramming, doing something once and then moving on is not likely to help you remember it in the long run. Practice makes perfect, and in studying, REVIEWING makes perfect!

REVIEWING MEANS GOING OVER INFORMATION THAT YOU'VE ALREADY LEARNED. THIS REPETITION HELPS MOVE THE INFORMATION IN YOUR BRAIN FROM SHORT-TERM MEMORY TO LONG-TERM MEMORY.

Reviewing can include going over old material before starting something new. It can be repetition of the same thing, such as a times table, every day for a week so you remember it by the end. Or it can be randomly repeating information or testing yourself to make sure it really sticks.

Things we've just learned are stored temporarily in SHORT-TERM memory.
When we repeat the information or link it to something we know, it transfers into LONG-TERM memory.
That means we'll still remember it days, or even MONTHS, LATER!

TOP TIPS TO REACH

Reviewing comes in lots of forms. You might read over your notes or rewrite them. You might review alone or with a friend. Try out these strategies to reach your reviewing goal:

1 REVIEW BEFORE YOU START

Each time you sit down to study, have a quick recap of what you last worked on. Read over your work and notes. This helps set it in your brain and gets you ready for learning something new.

2 REVIEW AT THE END OF THE WEEK

AT THE WEEKEND, THINK ABOUT WHAT YOU LEARNED IN THE PAST WEEK. REFLECT ON NEW TOPICS AND SKILLS.

YOUR REVIEWING GOAL

3 QUIZ YOURSELF

Test your knowledge of what you've learned. Quiz yourself with little questions. Even if you don't know an answer, finding it out will help you remember for the future.

4 USE A FRIEND

A FANTASTIC WAY TO GET NEW INFORMATION TO CLICK IS TO TEACH IT TO SOMEONE ELSE. TRYING TO EXPLAIN SOMETHING HELPS YOU MAKE SURE YOU UNDERSTAND IT YOURSELF AND SHOWS YOU THINGS YOU MIGHT HAVE FORGOTTEN. YOU AND A FRIEND COULD ALSO QUIZ EACH OTHER.

Reviewing can serve you well in other areas of your work too. Review instructions before you start a project or test to make sure you know what you're doing. Review the things you understand and those you don't so you know what to focus on.

Review, review, review!

You might want to take notes in class to remember what your teacher is saying. At home, try taking notes on information you read.

GOAL 6

SAY YES TO NOTES

How do you take notes? Do you write down everything you read and hear? Or do you focus on the moment and take down nothing? Find a happy balance somewhere in the middle to become a pro notetaker.

When you do take notes, there are a few tried and tested techniques to try:

SOME PEOPLE USE AN OUTLINE METHOD. THEY USE BULLET POINTS TO LIST HEADINGS AND KEY POINTS THAT FALL UNDER EACH.

Others use a VISUAL approach. If you think in pictures, you might like to take notes in pictures too. Draw images that help you remember what the teacher said, doodle lines and symbols to connect ideas ...

Make it work for the way you think.

Others use a NOTES UPON NOTES strategy. They take bullet-point notes in the main section of their page. Then they add summaries along the side and at the bottom. This helps pull out key info.

Everyone has their own way. The important thing is to find the one that works for you.

TOP TIPS TO WRITE TOP NOTES

As well as recording new information, the act of writing things down helps you remember them. Try these top tips to say yes to top notes:

SUPER STAR!

1 WRITE DOWN KEY POINTS

You don't need to write down EVERYTHING that you hear in class. Pick out the main points your teacher is saying.

2 USE YOUR OWN WORDS

IF YOU'RE TAKING NOTES ON A BOOK YOU'RE READING, TRY WRITING IMPORTANT INFORMATION IN YOUR OWN WORDS, RATHER THAN JUST COPYING IT DOWN. THIS HELPS MAKE SURE YOU'RE LEARNING AND UNDERSTANDING.

3 REVIEW THEM

DON'T JUST PUT YOUR NOTES ASIDE, NEVER TO BE SEEN AGAIN. READ BACK OVER THEM WHEN YOU REVIEW TO REMIND YOURSELF OF KEY INFORMATION.

4 REWRITE IF NECESSARY

After you've taken notes, read them over. Is anything missing? Unclear? Rewriting your notes can help fill in gaps and make them clearer too.

5 ORGANISE

USE NOTEBOOKS OR BINDERS TO KEEP YOUR NOTES SAFE. MAKE SURE YOU CAN EASILY FIND THEM WHEN YOU NEED THEM!

6 FIND YOUR GROOVE

You might find it easier to work on a tablet or computer, or you might prefer a paper notebook. Work out what's best for you.

GREAT STUFF!

HIT THE RIGHT NOTE!

GOAL 7

BREAK IT DOWN

IMAGINE TRYING TO BUILD A CAR ALL AT ONCE. It would be too much! Very quickly it might become overwhelming. But when engineers break a car down into parts, such as the wheels, engine, and body, it seems much more possible.

The same goes for studying. If you try to do everything all at once, you might get so overwhelmed that you end up doing nothing at all.

SOMETIMES IT'S HARD TO KNOW WHERE TO START WHEN YOU HAVE SOMETHING BIG TO DO. BREAKING IT DOWN HELPS YOU FIND SOMEWHERE – ANYWHERE! – TO BEGIN. EVEN IF YOU JUST DO A SMALL AMOUNT EACH DAY, YOU'VE MADE A DENT IN THE WORK.

If you've got lots of different subjects to work on, you can break them down, too. Suddenly, studying feels much more manageable.

TOP TIPS TO

Learn to break things down to build up your confidence. Try these extra tips to get to your break-it-down goal:

1 SPLIT IT INTO CHUNKS

If you've got a list of 50 spelling words to learn, don't try to do them all at once! Try learning five at a time. Get those five to stick before moving on to the next.

2 FOCUS ON ONE THING AT A TIME

YOU MIGHT HAVE A SCIENCE PROJECT, A SPELLING TEST, AND TIMES TABLES TO LEARN ALL IN ONE WEEK. NEVER FEAR! FOCUS ON ONE THING AT A TIME. THAT WAY EVERYTHING GETS THE ATTENTION IT DESERVES.

BREAK IT DOWN

3 GIVE EACH STUDY SESSION A GOAL

This should be just a small target to hit – such as learning 10 spelling words or one times table. Give yourself little goals each time you study, and you'll feel that you're making progress every time you achieve them.

4 COVER IT UP

IF A SHEET FULL OF MATH QUESTIONS IS TAUNTING YOU, COVER THEM UP! USE A PIECE OF PAPER TO COVER ALL BUT THE TOP QUESTION. THIS HELPS YOU PUT THE OTHERS OUT OF YOUR MIND AND FOCUS ON ONE AT A TIME.

Break it down ...
build it up!

GOAL 8

DON'T BE AFRAID OF MISTAKES

Do you spend the day being scared of monsters? Probably not. Do you spend the day fearing making mistakes?

If you said yes, think about why. What would be so bad if you made a mistake? You're not worried about monsters. Why worry about making mistakes?

Mistakes in tests, projects, and work are bound to happen. Remember, you've only just learned it! And if you knew everything already, there would be no point learning or studying at all.

IN FACT, MAKING MISTAKES CAN HELP WITH YOUR STUDYING:

Once you've made a mistake, you're aware of the wrong answer. You are more likely to remember this, and less likely to make the same mistake again.

MISTAKES ARE AN OPPORTUNITY TO LEARN SOMETHING NEW.

Mistakes remind us that nobody is perfect.

MISTAKES CAN SHOW YOU WHERE YOU COULD FOCUS YOUR STUDYING.

EVERYBODY makes mistakes. You just have to keep going. Make the most of it by learning from them.

TOP TIPS TO DEAL

The first step in this goal is admitting that mistakes are going to happen. The next step is embracing them! Try these strategies to achieve your goal and banish your fear of mistakes:

1 DON'T LET MISTAKES SLOW YOU DOWN

If you make a mistake, try not to let it frustrate you. Just keep going! Fix the error or skip it and go back to it later. Don't let it put you off your awesome studying.

2 MAKE MISTAKES ON PURPOSE

GET USED TO MAKING MISTAKES AND SEE HOW THEY CAN HELP YOU. TRY A QUIZ ON SOMETHING YOU DON'T KNOW ALL THAT WELL. GUESS THE ANSWERS – THEN SEE HOW WELL THAT HELPS YOU REMEMBER THEM FOR NEXT TIME!

WITH MISTAKES

3 OWN YOUR MISTAKES

When you make a mistake, turn it into a good thing. Find what you can learn from it. Does it help you remember an answer? Or maybe it gives you something new to add to your next study session?

4 FIND WAYS TO DEAL WITH THEM

IF YOU FIND YOURSELF GETTING FRUSTRATED BY MISTAKES, THINK ABOUT WHAT YOU CAN DO TO MOVE PAST THEM. TRY TAKING THREE DEEP BREATHS. THEN TRY AGAIN OR MOVE ON. LOOK BACK AT ALL THE WORK THAT YOU'VE DONE TO REMIND YOURSELF HOW FAR YOU'VE COME.

GOAL 9

FIND THE FUN

Can you think of a time when you were playing – and then realized you learned something? Like when your hair stood on end at the science museum, and you learned about electricity? Sometimes facts stick best when they're learned through **FUN.**

PRESCHOOLS HAVE BEEN USING THE CONCEPT OF LEARNING THROUGH FUN FOR AGES, WITH SAND TABLES, PAINTING, AND SONGS MAKING UP BIG PARTS OF THE DAY.

Even before any formal school, babies are learning words and actions from exploring their world and playing with the people around them.

THERE'S NO NEED TO GROW OUT OF THIS WAY OF LEARNING. YOU'RE MORE LIKELY TO REMEMBER SOMETHING IF YOU'RE INTERESTED IN IT, SO WHY NOT FIND THE FUN IN YOUR STUDYING?

It might be hard to get straight into doing homework after a big day of school, so look for new, fun ways to learn and revise.

MAKE GAMES OUT OF HOMEWORK, TALK ABOUT IDEAS WITH FAMILY AND FRIENDS, QUIZ EACH OTHER ... EVEN LINK YOUR WORK TO MOVIES YOU LIKE BY TALKING ABOUT THE MATH OR SCIENCE IN THEM. FIND THE FUN THAT GETS YOU EXCITED ABOUT STUDYING – AND HELPS IT STICK.

Make studying a game!

TOP TIPS TO FIND THE FUN

Everyone has different interests and different things that they enjoy. Try these games to find your own kind of fun in your studying:

1 LINK TO YOUR INTERESTS

Do you like video games, movies, or books? Make up stories about the characters or write book reports to work on your writing skills.

2 LINK TO EVERYDAY ACTIVITIES

YOU COULD TALK ABOUT FRACTIONS WHEN YOU'RE BAKING OR ADD UP COOKING TIMES WHEN YOU'RE COOKING. TRY TALKING ABOUT FOOD GROUPS OR THE DIGESTIVE SYSTEM WHEN YOU PLAN DINNER. THINK ABOUT OTHER WAYS TO BRING YOUR SCHOOLWORK INTO YOUR LIFE.

3 LINK TO GAMES

Every time you catch a ball, do a math problem. Or every time you make a move in a board game, recite a fact. Link learning with fun!

4 MAKE A PUZZLE

IF YOU'RE LEARNING SOMETHING VISUAL, SUCH AS GEOGRAPHY OR PARTS OF THE HUMAN BODY, YOU COULD PRINT OUT A PICTURE AND CUT IT INTO PUZZLE PIECES. PUT IT BACK TOGETHER AND LEARN WHILE YOU'RE COMPLETING IT!

5 WRITE OUT FLASHCARDS

Write a question on the front and an answer on the back of each card. Have them ready to whizz through on your own or with family or friends. For an extra challenge, you could try timing yourself and work to beat your score the next time.

GOAL 10

GIVE YOURSELF A BREAK

Just as your body needs a rest after physical exercise, your mind needs a break after a mental workout.

If you're tired, frustrated, or angry, no matter how hard you try you just won't achieve the same quality of studying as when you're in a clearer frame of mind. So take a break.

Taking a step back can help clear your mind so it's ready to study when you are.

PLANNING BREAKS INTO YOUR SCHEDULE GIVES YOU TARGETS TO WORK TOWARDS.

Taking a break reminds you to go easy on yourself! It allows you to reflect on how far you've come.

A BREAK CAN IMPROVE YOUR MOOD.

Having a rest can give you the energy to focus and concentrate on your work again.

YOUR BRAIN CAN SOMETIMES CONTINUE TO PROCESS INFORMATION WHILE YOU'RE NOT FORCING IT.

When you go back to work after a break, you might see a problem in a whole new light and come up with a brand new solution.

A **break** can be just as important as study time. Pause, refresh, and rejuvenate – and your studying will see the **difference**!

TOP TIPS TO

A break doesn't need to be long – just enough to calm your mind so you can focus properly on your studying. Sometimes your body will tell you it's time to step away, and other times you might want to plan in some downtime. Try these techniques to find your inner peace:

1 TAKE DEEP BREATHS

CLOSE YOUR EYES AND FOCUS ON YOUR BREATH. SLOWLY BREATHE IN .... AND OUT. TAKE 10 OF THESE DEEP BREATHS BEFORE YOU GO BACK TO WORK.

2 GO FOR A WALK

Getting outside is one of the best things you can do for your mind. Walk away from your work and focus on nature.

3 PLAY OR DO EXERCISE

TAKE YOUR MIND OFF ANY FRUSTRATIONS, THEN COME BACK FEELING REFRESHED!

TAKE A BREAK

4 DAYDREAM

If you have trouble switching off, learn to let your mind wander. Find a quiet place, stare into space, and just daydream.

5 SCHEDULE IN BREAKS

THINK ABOUT HOW YOU WORK. MAYBE YOU CAN DO HALF AN HOUR OF SOLID STUDYING BEFORE YOUR MIND BEGINS TO WANDER. SO MAKE A STUDY SCHEDULE THAT GIVES YOU A BREAK AFTER 30 MINUTES.

Break it to make it!

6 REWARD YOURSELF

You could simply reward yourself with positive thoughts about what you've accomplished, or treat yourself to a fun activity when you've done a good session.

GLOSSARY

BULLET POINTS - Symbols indicating each section in a list of information.

CADDY - A holder in which you can organize the things you need for studying and carry them about.

CRAM - To study a lot in a short space of time.

DEADLINE - The date that something needs to be done by.

DISTRACTION - Something that takes your attention away from the task you're doing.

DOWNTIME - Time when you are resting and relaxing rather than studying.

FOCUS - To pay particular attention to something.

HABIT - Something that you do regularly, which is often automatic and done without you thinking about it much.

INGRAINED - Firmly fixed inside something.

LONG-TERM MEMORY: The ability to store and remember information over a long period of time.

MENTAL - To do with the mind.

OVERWHELMED: Feeling a huge weight from too many things to do or too much pressure.

PORTABLE - Able to be picked up and moved around easily.

PRACTICAL - Realistic and sensible for a real-world situation.

PRIORITY - Something of top importance.

PROCRASTINATE - To put off doing something.

REJUVENATE - To give something or someone more energy.

REVIEWING - Going over something again carefully.

SCHEDULES - Lists of dates by which you are aiming to get things done.

SHORT-TERM MEMORY - The ability to store and remember information for a short amount of time.

STRATEGIES - Plans you make to help you achieve your goals.

SUMMARIES - Shorter pieces of writing summing up the main points of something.

FURTHER INFORMATION

WEBSITES:

www.bbc.co.uk/bitesize – a website full of information, games, and quizzes on all topics linked to your learning in school.

www.kidshealth.org/en/kids/studying.html – Nemours KidsHealth is a group focused on improving kids' health and offering the support needed to do so. This webpage gives useful tips on smart studying.

www.hachettechildrens.co.uk – the Franklin Watts and Wayland pages contain links to activities and worksheets to support children's learning.

BOOKS:

Exam Attack by Nicola Morgan, 2020, Franklin Watts

Help Your Kids with Study Skills by Carol Vorderman, 2016, DK

Life Skills by Keilly Swift, 2021, DK

The 7 Habits of Happy Kids by Sean Covey, 2008, Simon & Schuster

INDEX